CW00738794

CONCORDE

AN ICON IN THE NEWS

CONCORDE

AN ICON IN THE NEWS

mirrorpix

The
History
Press

Cover Illustrations. **Front:** A farmer watches as Concorde comes in to land after breaking the sound barrier for the first time. **Back:** Concorde 002 and the team that put it together.

First published 2019

The History Press
The Mill, Brimscombe Port
Stroud, Gloucestershire, GL5 2QG
www.thehistorypress.co.uk

© Mirrorpix, 2019

The right of Mirrorpix to be identified as the Author
of this work has been asserted in accordance with the
Copyright, Designs and Patents Act 1988.

British Library Cataloguing in Publication Data.
A catalogue record for this book is available from the British Library.

ISBN 978 0 7509 8910 7

Typesetting and origination by The History Press
Printed and bound in India by Thomson Press India Ltd

INTRODUCTION

On 2 March 1969, Concorde took off from Toulouse for what was described as a 'faultless' maiden test flight. The flight lasted just 27 minutes, but it flew Concorde into history as surely the most iconic airliner of all time – as beloved by the fortunate travellers on board as by the masses who regularly gathered below, casting eyes upwards hoping for a glimpse of that famous profile.

Concorde enjoyed an exceptional career, but disaster struck with the tragic Paris crash in 2000. After that, it seemed that the world was changing and Concorde's days were numbered. Retired in 2003, its emotive last flight paid tribute to the end of an era.

This collection of photographs follows Concorde's story through the eyes of the media, who documented every move from construction to final journey. Charting significant events in Concorde's lifetime, whether breaking the sound barrier or taking part in the jubilee celebratory flypast, it also features many passengers, well-known faces and lucky competition winners. These stunning photographs from the Mirrorpix archives look back over the career of a marvellous aircraft.

↑ **May 1964:** The hunt for the perfect shape. These thirteen wind tunnel models helped engineers perfect the Concorde's design.

↑ **February 1967**: Inside Concorde Prototype 2.

→ **March 1967:**
Concorde being built
in Bristol, England.

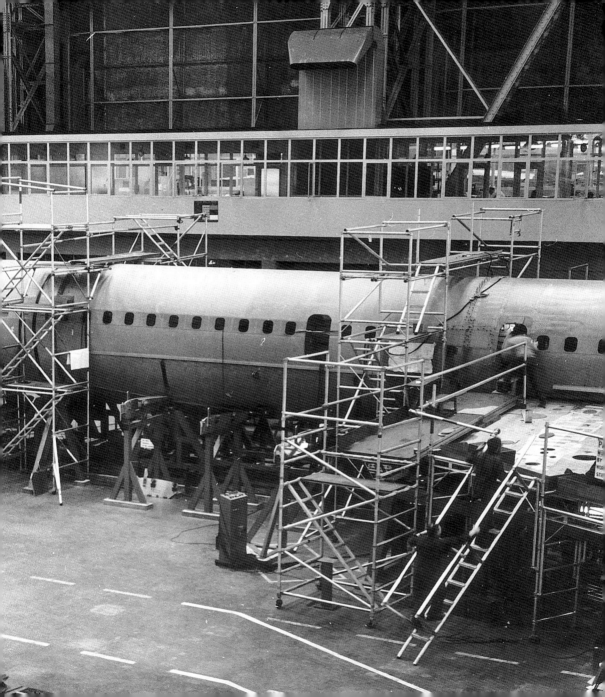

↑ **March 1967**: Engineers at the Bristol Siddeley factory working on the Rolls-Royce Olympus engine, the power behind Concorde.

→ **May 1967**: Francine Girgnon (29) from Air Canada arrives in London this morning to be one of the first hostesses.

↓ **Monday 11 December 1967:** Prototype 001 makes its first official public appearance as it is unveiled from its Sud Aviation hanger in Toulouse, France.

→ The Concorde 001 in the hangar at Toulouse.

It was a quiet coming-out affair for Concorde 002 on Thursday, 12 September 1968. There was no fuss as the British prototype of the Anglo-French supersonic airliner was towed for the first time from its British Aircraft Corporation hangar at Filton, Bristol. Both the British and French governments have asked the manufacturers on both sides of the Channel to investigate how quickly production can be increased to meet an expected body of sales.

→ Concorde was then towed to engine testing area, with panels of an aluminium acoustic material over its tail and rear fuselage to protect its surfaces during engine runs.

18   CONCORDE

↑ The British Concorde 002 and the French 001 are identical twins. Although assembled several hundred miles apart in two countries, each contains exactly the same French- and British-built parts.

↑ Walter Cowley and Stanley Barrington, technicians at RAE Bedford, carry out the model of Concorde.

Toulouse Airport, France, Sunday, 2 March 1969: the French-built Concorde 001 takes to the skies for the first time. Test pilot André Turcat is at the controls for the maiden flight, going up to 10,000ft at speeds of up to 300mph during a 28-minute flight.

↑ Security at perimeter of airport.

↑ Lift off!

↑ Concorde lands after a successful flight. The mechanism in the tail shows that the parachute has been deployed and released from the rear of aircraft.

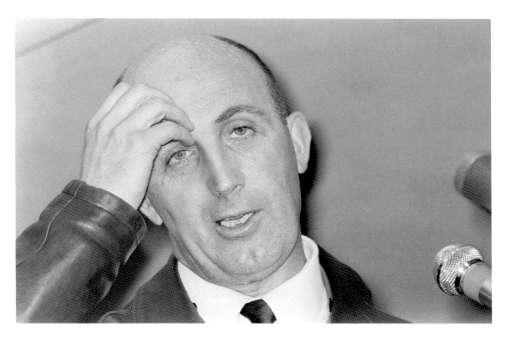

↑ André Turcat at a press conference.

The British-built Concorde 002 takes to the skies just over a month later, on 9 April 1969. The 21-minute maiden flight is piloted by chief BAC test pilot Brian Trubshaw and co-pilot John Cochrane, and concludes with a perfect landing at RAF Fairford, Gloucestershire.

↑ A perfect landing.

→ Approaching the runway at Filton after its maiden flight.

↑ The Queen enjoys the flypast with Prince Philip and younger members of the Royal Family. The children are (left to right) Viscount Linley, Prince Edward and James Ogilvy (son of Princess Alexandra and the Hon. Angus Ogilvy).

← 14 June 1969: Pictured from the roof of the *Sunday Mirror*, Concorde is on its way to salute the Queen at the Trooping of the Colour.

↑ → **14 August 1970**: Concorde lands at RAF Fairfield after a successful test flight of its new engines, breaking the sound barrier for the first time.

↑ **7 September 1970**: Concorde makes its first appearance at the Farnborough Air Show, flying low over the spectators.

→ **December 1970**: The team who got Concorde 002 off the ground.

↑ **1 January 1971:** Dr Archibald Russell, the retiring chairman of the British Aircraft Corporation's Filton Division, and the designer of Concorde, with his personal model of Concorde.

→ **May 1971:** Captain Brian Trubshaw, the first British man to fly Concorde, after being presented with the Air League Founders' Medal.

← **12 January 1972:** The Duke of Edinburgh is to fly Concorde 002 at Mach Two – twice the speed of sound – over the Bay of Biscay. The flight was delayed for more than three hours when a fault developed in the braking system.

→ **February 1972:** Buy your own Concorde for 53p (but not the one at the back). Corgi Toys' model Concordes line up with 001.

↑ **10 May 1972**: Concorde worker Adrian Pollicutt commutes from Filton, England, to Toulouse, France. Here he is with David Bradley and Concorde in the background.

↑ **19 May 1972:** Prime Minister Edward Heath meets Concorde.

← 1 July 1972: Concorde returns to Heathrow after sales world tour. Brian Trubshaw, Chief Test Pilot, and Michael Heseltine, Minister for Aerospace after the flight.

↑ Michael Heseltine and Brian Trubshaw at the press conference after the flight.

↑ **3 July 1972:** Concorde on show at Heathrow Airport.

↑ **8 September 1972**: Blackpool comes to a standstill as Concorde flies over; every vantage point occupied for a glimpse of the plane.

On 23 October 1973, Concorde 002 flew an 83-minute test-flight over the Bay of Biscay, during which the plane went supersonic for 38 minutes. Among the passengers on the flight are Princess Anne and her fiancé Captain Mark Phillips – Anne's dream was to fly in the plane.

↑ The test-flight ended at Fairford, Gloucestershire.

↑ Princess Anne and test pilot Brian Trubshaw, after leaving the plane.

→ **March 1974:** The production line of Concorde at BAC's works in Filton. Pictured here are the fourth and sixth aircraft to be made for BOAC.

↑ **May 1974:** Three Concorde workers (with their own style of headwear) at the entrance to Downing Street. Workers from the factories in Bristol and Weybridge descended upon Downing Street to demonstrate and present petitions to ministers, who were attending a Cabinet meeting that would decide the plane's future.

↑ **1 September 1974**: Prototype 101 comes in to land with nose drooped and undercarriage lowered at the Farnborough Air Show.

54   CONCORDE

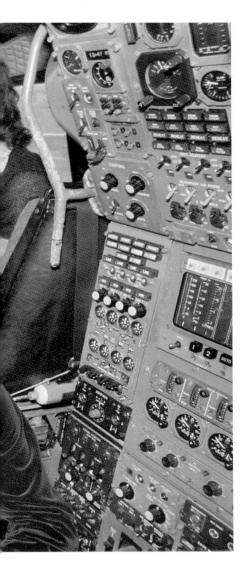

← **January 1975:** The pop group Pilot with Concorde at Fairford.

← **January 1975:** The pop group Pilot with Concorde at Fairford.

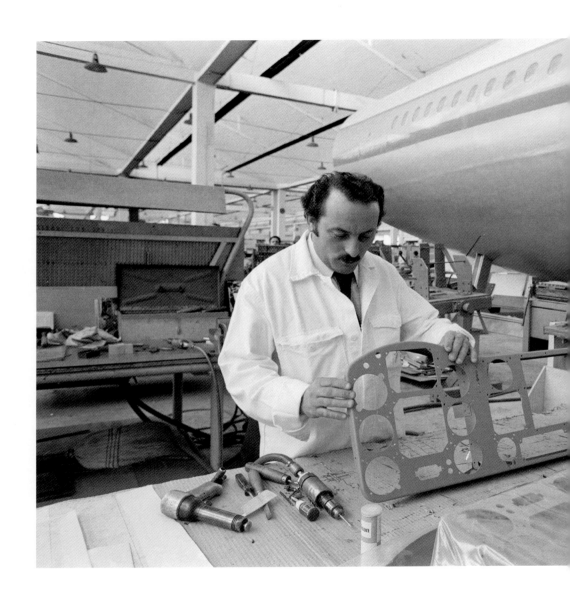

← **22 April 1975:** Mr Irene Quaranta pictured at work in the Toulouse Aircraft factory in Southern France.

↑ 14 January 1976: Hardy Amies has designed the uniform for the British Airways cabin crew. For supersonic travel the designers have taken quite a revolutionary approach, allowing the individual to choose from a variety of garments in two colours.

← 24 August 1975: Thirty-five guests of British Airways, selected at random by computer ballot, took a three-and-a-half-hour, 5,000-mile round trip over the Atlantic as part of the plane's certification programme. Nigel Barnes of Caversham, Reading, holds up his ticket for the flight before boarding the plane at Heathrow.

On 21 January 1976, seven years after the maiden test flight, the inaugural commercial flights of Concorde took off simultaneously at 11.40 a.m. One left Heathrow Airport, London, to fly to Bahrain in the Middle East as the other, an Air France flight, took off from Orly Airport, Paris, for Rio De Janeiro via Dakar, Senegal.

←↑ The British Concorde being loaded at Heathrow Airport, ahead of its inaugural flight to Bahrain.

↑ Passenger Bob Ingham, who saved for three years for his plane ticket, pictured at Heathrow in the outfit he designed to do justice to the aircraft he worships.

← Passengers queuing up to check in.

← Ramp Liaison Officer Barbara Johnson, who is responsible for the plane's departure.

→ The British Airways flight just after taking off from London.

← **4 February 1976**: Concorde flies through fog and snow in London, en route to the warmer climate of Bahrain.

↓ **2 March 1976**: Six-month-old Kathy Frith is believed to be the first baby to fly supersonic.

↑ **24 May 1976:** Check in at London Airport.

↑ **June 1976**: Prime Minister James Callaghan, with Chancellor Denis Healey and Foreign Secretary Anthony Crosland, boarding Concorde at Heathrow.

→ **20 August 1977:** Concorde 101 touches down at its final home at Duxford, Cambridge. Brian Trubshaw brought it safely into land, where it was greeted by a cheering crowd.

It had not been easy or straightforward. With the aircraft's test career over, 101 had been donated to the Duxford Aviation Society, who were eagerly awaiting its arrival. But first, a few problems had to be overcome. The runway at Duxford was too short, so weight needed to be lost from the plane, but contractors were also about to remove a third of the runway to make way for the M11. Time was of the essence.

→ Spectators sit on the wing of a Dan Air Comet 4 to get the perfect picture of Concorde as she taxis into the apron at Duxford.

↑ **3 November 1977:** The Queen and the Duke of Edinburgh disembarking following their flight from Barbados. They had been visiting the West Indies as part of the Queen's Commonwealth Silver Jubilee tour.

↑ **August 1978:** Gary Jones of Sussex, dressed as Concorde, at this year's National Birdman Rally on Bognor Regis Pier.

↑ **1 November 1978:** Uri Geller at London Airport with a Concorde.

→ **12 February 1979:** The Queen and Prince Philip leaving Heathrow Airport at the start of her Middle East Tour.

→ Royal cargo safely on board, Concorde prepares to leave Heathrow in the snow.

↑ **30 November 1979**: Concorde flying at night.

→ **December 1979**: With an ear-splitting roar, Concorde thunders over the rooftops.

← **21 June 1980:** Concorde crew.

↑ **11 October 1980:** Eight members of the Royal Flying Corps went on a two-hour flight from Heathrow with the Concorde Appreciation Society. Among them were cap-swapper Eric Hoylands, 87, from Middlestown, West Yorks; Concorde Captain Monty Burton (wearing a First World War flying helmet); and Robert Corkling, 86, of West Sussex.

→ **11 January 1982:** Doctor Who star Peter Davison came face to face with Concorde today when the Doctor's travels took him to Heathrow Airport.

↑ **27 August 1982:** Pilot Jock Lowe with Concorde at Newcastle Airport.

→ **20 December 1982:** Keith Richards, guitarist with the Rolling Stones, preparing to board with his then girlfriend Patti Hansen.

↑ **29 August 1983:** Happy passengers about to board at Newcastle Airport.

← ↑ **30 August 1983:** British Airways launches its Super Shuttle Service, where passengers will fly from London to Glasgow on Concorde.

↑ → **9 September 1983:** Hundreds of people were drenched by heavy rain as they pulled Concorde around an airfield at the end of a rope. They were making a record-breaking attempt to raise money for disabled children. The idea came from the Wickford Rotary Club, the plane from the static display aircraft exhibition at the Imperial War Museum, Duxford.

↑ **3 December 1983:** Four Americans flew over on Concorde just to buy Cabbage Patch Dolls from London's Hamleys toystore.

→ **31 July 1984:** Frank Sinatra and his wife Barbara Marx at Heathrow Airport, prior to departing for New York aboard Concorde.

← **25 August 1984:** Winners of a *Sunday Sun* competition to win a flight on Concorde. From left to right: Glenis Nixon, flight engineer Bill Brown, and Margaret Heckels.

↑ **27 August 1984:** Keith Bell and Isabel Beckwith – winners of an *Evening Chronicle* competition – celebrate as they prepare to board.

→ **27 August 1984:** More winners of the *Evening Chronicle* competition – from left to right: Fiona Raine, Unity Morris, Gavin Allan, Michael Robson and Chris Bryant.

↑ **25 April 1985:** Concorde at Heathrow.

↑ **13 July 1985:** Singer Phil Collins and his then wife Jill Tavelman about to board a Concorde flight to the USA, so Phil can perform at the JFK Stadium in Philadelphia.

← **2 April 1986:** Excited passengers in the cockpit.

← ↑ **2 April 1986:** Happy passengers on Concorde.

← **2 April 1986:** Granny's trip on Concorde.

↑ **2 April 1986:** Passengers posing in front of Concorde.

↑ **3 April 1986:** Mick Jagger at Heathrow, about to leave on Concorde with his partner Jerry Hall and family.

→ **14 April 1986:** Princess Diana departing on Concorde from Heathrow to Vienna.

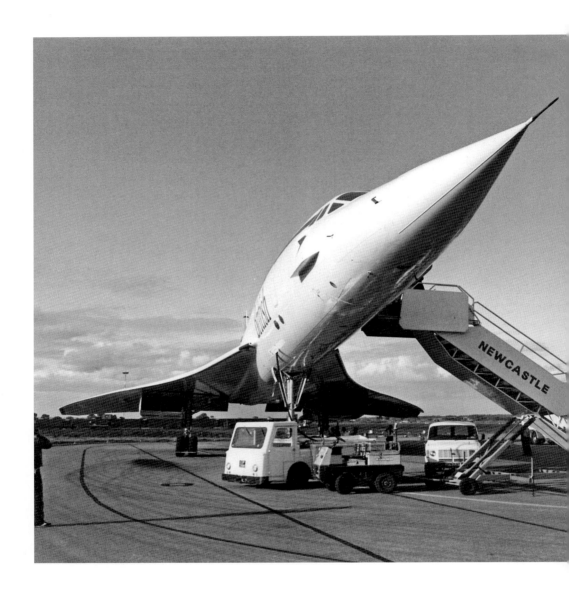

← **10 December 1986:** A British Airways Concorde visits Newcastle Airport.

↑ **July 1986:** Golfer Greg Norman holds the Claret Jug trophy after winning the British Open, alongside Concorde pilot John Cook.

→ **22 November 1987:** Celebrating Concorde's tenth birthday.

→ **21 January 1988:** Elton John with then wife Renate Blauel and friends (including Ringo Starr) about to board.

On the cheque:

BARCLAYS

27th January 1988

Pay THE COMIC RELIEF FUND,
Five Thousand, Three Hundred
and Twenty Five pounds. TOBY RESTAURANTS.

£5,325

or order

← ↑ **27 January 1988:** Red Nose Day on Concorde.

↑ **7 August 1994:** Concorde comes in for landing at Newcastle Airport.

→ **24 April 1994:** 13-year-old David Taylor of Ponteland takes the co-pilot seat next to captain Alan Harkness.

↑ **17 November 2014:** Norman Dawson, a retired British Airways engineer, shows off his to-scale models of a 747 jumbo jet and Concorde – made with 10,000 matches!

← **19 January 1996:** Engineer Paul Snelgrove gives Concorde a polish on its twentieth birthday.

↑ **25 September 1990:** Rod Hull and Emu on the flight deck with a Venture Scout.

↑ **1980:** Concorde in Singapore Airlines livery.

↑ **1 July 1991**: Richard Branson has hijacked a British Airways' Concorde model and changed the livery to Virgin.

→ **December 1993**: Father Christmas and his reindeer greet Concorde upon its arrival in Finnish Lapland.

↑ **24 April 1994:** Crowds watch the arrival of the Concorde.

↑ **7 August 1994:** Crowds gather to look at the plane on arrival at Newcastle Airport.

↑ **19 January 1996:** Concorde's twentieth birthday is celebrated with champagne and a cake by twenty support staff at Heathrow Airport.

← **2 April 1996:** Air France have painted one of their Concordes in the colours of Pepsi's new cans – Cindy Crawford, Andre Agassi and Claudia Schiffer are at the launch.

↑ → **17 July 2001:** The British Airways Concorde takes off for the first time since the Paris crash the previous year, flying from Heathrow.

↑ **July 2001:** A test flight at Brize Norton.

↑ **June 2002**: Concorde and the Red Arrows fly over Buckingham Palace in celebration of Queen Elizabeth II's Golden Jubilee.

← ↑ → 24 October 2003: Concorde's final commercial flights; actress Jodie Kidd and former *Daily Mirror* editor Piers Morgan disembark.

← **26 November 2003:** Concorde touches down at Filton Airfield today for the last time in its forty-year history.

↑ **18 January 2016:** Scotland's Concorde was the first aircraft in the BA fleet to begin commercial passenger flights when she flew from London Heathrow to Bahrain on 21 January 1976. On board was a haggis bound for the country's Scots community for their Burns Night celebrations. Today, as a celebration of forty years, a haggis will be piped on board the Concorde at the National Museum of Flight, and a museum staff member will recite a specially composed version of Burns' 'Address to a Haggis'.